Resilience

Dear Linda

With love

Mary

4/2007

More Praise for Resilience:

"Vivid descriptions of everyday life: an ordinary magic!"
Marc Renzoni, school psychologist

"Her words plumb the sensuous underpinnings of the every day. There she creates magical worlds out of the dust and bones of experience. She makes the common alive, new."
Linda Drajem, PhD, poet, teacher

"I love these poems! They give me inspiration...." **Bette Morris, poet, psychotherapist**

"Chiseled writing that softens our human shards." **Kathleen Shoemaker, poet**

"Norris' writing is, by turns, wild yet grounded, sensitive and strong. There is so much future in it." **Timothy Maggio, CRC, psychotherapist, writer**

"Norris celebrates her imagination: she fearlessly spins exquisite imagery and blends insights from daily life, archetype, and dream into lyrical language, her poems' sure cloth. Norris dares us to imagine the circles we may share in our human, molecular dance." **Jimmie Gilliam, author of Rime and Roar of Revolution, Ain't No Bears Out Tonight, and Pieces of Bread**

And More Praise for Resilience:

"She will take you on a journey through sapphire air, across emerald hills, so hold on! Your own face will be clearer in the mirror." **Barbara Faust, poet, teacher**

"Norris transports us to a different world. There you can smell the damp undergrowth, feel the quiet night, take a peek inside. Her lyrics have physical impact. They make you think and they make you sweat." **Madeline Davis, author, Boots of Leather, Slippers of Gold**

"Quixotic and luminous, Marjorie Norris' poetry delights the ear and the heart. Her themes encompass the life cycle with particular emphasis on women's redemption." **Margaret Cusack, author, Teaching to Learn: Reflections on Risk-Taking in an Elementary Classroom**

"We are brought back to an early place where all is promise. Norris' work offers us this wonder." **Michael Villar, teacher**

"A hunter-gatherer of language, following memory into magical places, she stalks the rare observation, the endangered feeling, the raw experience from which she creates these poems, wise and tender." **Kathleen Betsko Yale, editor, Interviews with Comtemporary Women Playwrights, playwright, ABC-TV Theatre Award, best original play script: "Johnny Bull"**

Resilience

poems

Marjorie Norris

Aventine Press

Aventine Press
1023 4th Avenue, Suite 204
San Diego, CA 92101

ISBN: 1-59330-452-8

Printed in the United States of America

Preface: To the Women of the Crooked Circle, my long-lived writing group

Your stems are lovely,
    Dark and deep
    But I have promises
    To keep
And miles to go before I sleep

        --Marjorie Norris
        (with thanks to Robert Frost)

The South

O Great Spirit of the south,
Protector of the fruitful land,
And of all green and growing things,
The noble trees and grasses,
Grandmother Earth, Soul of Nature,
Great power of the receptive,
Of nurturance and endurance,
Power to grow and bring forth
Flowers of the field,
Fruits of the garden

We pray that we may be aligned with you,
So that our power may flow through us,
For the good of this planet Earth,
And all living beings upon it

    --Native American blessing

Introduction:

Do you know what it is you're looking for? It is vibrantly alive, yet has no root or stem. You can't gather it up, you can't scatter it to the winds. The more you search for it the further away it gets. But don't search for it and it's right before your eyes, the miraculous sound always in your ears.—Zen Master Rinzai

This is my third book, following Chautauqua Breathing (2004), and Two Suns, Two Moons (2005). These poems are meant to show how life surprises us: seeds, stems, blooms. In roots of love, war, and trials we find the strength to hold our borrowed dreams, the generations.

I dedicate this book to three Muses: Linda Lavid, my writing friend and mentor, Anne Ritenour, a source of worldly resilience and Sally Johnson, whose eye sees it all in pictures. May your creative lives be blessed on the journey.

Table of Contents:

Dandelions

I met her, Laura, when she was three
She gave me the stolid brown-eyed
Look I'd always remember, and
Winged toward the back garden,
There drowning in dandelions,
Up to her knees and little hips,
Her blond hair flying like a soft
Nest for some small round bird
To land in, she comforted
Everything, her mother,
From Scotland, proud
And laughing

Grass

Is sprouting up, under
The blue U.S. mailbox
On the corner of Water Street
(on any corner in Mudville)
Skateboarders are flipping now
Their knees push down
To create a sky-born coast,
A flash to ground, a slap
To earth

Secret

You are a garden unknown, hidden away
Among the high grasses, I reach for your stems,
Your roots, you open up, a wildflower

It is your chin mostly and your elbow
I want to touch, leading you out onto
The planet, I want to show you how
Vital the world is, how warm, how
Experiential is the terrain, how inviting
The earth

And today I feel so mellow on this
World's rim, sinking my toes into
The sandy ground where cucumbers
And peppers, green, spring up like
Sprigs, sorrel, rosemary

I want to grow you like a culture
Water you and feed your heart
Draw from the sweet soil, then
Eat you from your soul's whispering:
Honeysuckle, cilantro, wild cardamom

Elbow

Once cracked
The heart learns
Nothing, leans
On its elbow
Drinking a beer
In a little dive
With tawdry dancers,
Others divested
On quests and
Other insurgents,
Other Don Quixotes,
Sancho Panzas

And the elbow
Flexes its bone,
Allows for muscle
On either side,
Is more resilient
That that feisty
Slab that throbs
Anonymously
Around the issue
Of love

Oh, elbow,
I yearn to go
Where you go,
Lean where you
Lean

Damsel in Distress

She is attracted, then
Repelled, by the dragon's
Fire. Should she stand
Along-side the dragon
So as not to get burned?
What blows is the wind,
Catching the animal's breath:
All things are consumed
When they are ready,
She muses

Heart

They say the heart learns nothing,
Bends over rice and macaroni
And steams. Good for the heart's
Complexion, increases pressure
And joie de vivre, this egoless
Zen steaming, this light dreaming,
And then the words weave. The
Heart fast forwards to find
Herself, slows to learn of her
Rejection

Grief

I leave behind these autumn droppings,
Oak leaves twirling next to maples, and
The golden lie that shrouds the ground
In its own orange and red vibrato.
Too much covered, I say, peeking
Out only occasionally to reveal
My own lost wantonness, there!
I said it, how I shed lives like needles
As they softened the ground below me,
The very soil I walked on

Love, What is It?

Oh, love can meander like an eel
In smooth waters, like a woolly sheep
On the mountain, loves come in
Soft packages of silk, then disruption
Breaks through like a volcano under
The water, love touches the bottom
And the top, foaming the sail's blade

And loves smells like vanilla, I can vouch
For it: I buy body oil in scents of vanilla/
The street vendor sells it (from the trunk
Of his car)/I purchase love again and again,
Putting kisses on my temples, my neck,
The backs of my knees/when love works,
It smells like vanilla

Beggar Girl

I always wanted a name,
She said, up till now,
No one has given me
This right. What will
You name me? I will
Name you Green Sadness,
Because you are like
The pulse of spring
That pushes up sharp,
Taut and pungent,
Not that you need
Such poignancy, but I
Can smell you there,
See you, hear you,
Feel your tremulous
Ache—I'll show you
Your face, the dark one
At the center of yourself

"Who made the batter, until I was molded?"
-author unknown

I love these women as much as family,
We sit here in a December rain,
A downpour and it wets us,
We tell stories of fear and
Jubilation, of hesitation,
Beauty and exploitation, underneath
There are stories that tried to destroy us,
Our limpid little girl
Arms that hugged a cat or knock-knees that chased the
Sparrows, the free part that felt invincible,
Ineffable yet
True, and all along our yards there were ruts where other
Girls paraded to be molded,
Our white anklets nylon and shaping
Our calves, our Mary Janes seriously conventional,
Our big bows,
Blue or red, bobbing on top of our heads,
Held by a barrette,
Or better yet, an urgent plea **not to make waves**,
The way we'd
Learn that cowards could try to own us. I am here to say
I have come through the most outrageous conditioning
Of families, it is what makes me sweat still at Christmas,
A cold dampness felt in the heart

Resolve

Hunger can make you restless
There's something in the belly
That grinds, doesn't fit
It's the empty spot
That sorrow fills
Then it runs over
Into loneliness
And off
Into dark ponds
Where willows wind
Spanish moss hangs
And owls look down

Soon you are in a canoe
Gliding, stuffing down
Sandwiches of egg salad
And pickles, olives, ripe
Apples, sipping coffee
From an old jug (as if
This lunch were made
By your Grandmother
Placed before you specially
Wrapped in linens,
A lacquered basket)

Then, your back unbent,
You are paddling, gliding
Away from your pain,
Once you've eaten,
You can see how hunger
Made your body tired,
Soul-weary, but filled
You with bright mettle,
A glib tongue:
Hunger formed you.
It took you on
Down the river

Tangerine

Was her hair on Christmas morning
The promise of something lavish
Pitted indentures tropical, the nipple
Of the stem and then the skin pulls
Freely, loosely around the juicy
Center, tangy zest, its white spray
Each orange moon falls wide
Like happiness, creates a mandala
That sits lunar in a blue sky bowl,
Watery indigo holds this clementine
In sweet eclipse, grasps her, grounds
Her, says Yes and Taste Me, once
More. Yes and Yes. More.

Hermit
   --to Kathy Shoemaker

I am seeded, troughed
In this little apartment
Where I live, now growing
Soft as a hermit crab, no
Shell, letting poems hit
Like a lightning bolts,
Welcome hail

One day, talking with you
On the phone, my lone-glazed
Eye, bright with the detached
Dimmed look of old saints, views
A hawk on the waterspout next
Door who hunkers over himself,
He washes his bright young
Feathers of copper and ecru,
Picks at himself as if remembering
A place before his birth, lifts
His taloned feet—washes them
In the spout, he is without
Guise or consciousness

Like me, he is only himself

Found Poem

He looked ancient,
Like one of the Eight
Holy Immortals,
A smart old god...
When he moved
Too slowly
For the work,
He packed his stuff
Into a brown
Shopping bag,
Walked down the road,
And flagged down
A Greyhound bus
Heading south
To San Francisco

(Bone, Fae Myenne Ng, 1993)

Of Oceans, Seas

She dreams of oceans, seas,
The deep mermaids who call her,
She can only go overboard,
There is no other direction
On this map, and the crags
Call, and the air swells,
And the boats list,
And the lovers swoon,
And it is all about the sea,
The dream, the longed-for
One, the yearning beneath.
For the mother holds the world,
And it keeps spinning and circling,
Despite the illusion of stillness
The child feels in her hands

Does a lone star twinkle by itself?
Or does the mother bend it, its little
Corners pointing, painting the soul's
Direction, the fierce anatomy
Of the skies, mahogany backdrop
To the world?

It takes generations to know a family's
Power, the mother's wish for the child,
That chiseled brilliance, the way
The heavens and earth will work it.
Like deep clay, the child becomes her
Own, her own mutation, the earth
And sky will build her, the sea water
Her, filling in each feature, each fissure
Responding

Memory

I remember, I remember
The glacées, the ice cream
So sweet, the jubilant
Sun coming up and on the grass,
The praise of summer days,
Phlox and wildflowers,
Petunias and the face
Of the pansy brown and gold,
Purple and yellow

Natasha

"Today feels like forever and yet/how still the leaves
lie"—Ruth Stone

Today feels like forever and yet
The sun languishes at twilight
In its purply tones of rose and repose
The rabbit freezes on the snow's crust
Pointing like an omen

Today I learn my friend
Divorced two years
Is to marry again
And I wonder if she's ready
Or throwing up her arms,
Her hopes

What would it be like
To live with an astronomer?
To see the vaulted skies
As worlds, to dabble
In a kind of dreamy infinity?

I write to her immediately
To send out two Chinese
Bowls, blue as skies
Sweet as robins' eggs or stars

All the while wondering
If she's centered, a personal sun,
Light. She is tender:
She feels just like a daughter

Core

The seeds are clinging to the axis
The deep stalky wood
And all around
Is core

Core in the neighborhood

Core of apple, core of the vine,
Core of the heart, your core or mine

Core of the city, core of the field
Core of the fruit, once skin is peeled

Core of my eyesight, core of your wish
Core of the poets in their words' petri dish

Core of the runner, core of the park
Seeds of the summer, song in the dark

Core of the moon surrounded by stars
Core of Venus and core of Mars

Core of the winter when I found you in snow
Core of the garden where all the ferns grow

And most of all now, in sun's early set
Core of sadness, core of "not yet"

People are Food
   --to the poet Wanda Coleman

People are food, I nibble on their knees
Gobble the experience of Wanda and
Her train ride, a drama seeking paradise:
She's headed to a fruited punchbowl,
Sweet taste of grape and mint, passion flowers

People are food, I digest all their little habits
Their sweetmeats, stews and all their blurred
Romances, silent meetings at smoky restaurants
People are food!

People are like beaded bags we carry to a party
Flashing the fire of sequins, rhinestones
Their eyes containing secrets, small change
And wild desire, the occasional bet on the big lotto:
Like beaded bags you can lure them out, out
From the back of their respective closets

Oh, people are like heaven, warm and loafy
Arms big as fresh bread, crusty joints and bakery
Calves planted firmly in platform shoes on the oak
Floors of renegade poets, occasional moisture collects
At a top lip, the smile tinged with the sweet smell
Of clove, there's a hint of lipstick left, somewhat
Chewed—oh, it's the forbidden truth of a woman
PEOPLE ARE FOOD!

Words

Look these words up—
I find them laughable:
Jacaranda
Bougainvillea
Arbor vitae
And persimmon

Let me laugh and laugh
At the sounds of these words
As when I smile at the message
You give when I don't under-
Stand a word you say

Speak to me
In another language

(This one) (You know)
(Is not working)

Instinct: A Joycean Childhood

I saw my sisters and my grandmother
Weeping from the long willows
The fronds unfolding
Like blue fingers strumming
On a waxy guitar
The grasses were calling
Wild so wild
Like tufts rising
To meet the greasy air
And I a little girl with auburn
Curls had an open stare: could
Only sing a melody to push
Myself, Tum-de-lum, La-la-loo
While sorting the sifting sands
Of the mud lot that skirted
That post-war house, a brown
Pleat dug into the earth to make
A plate to imaginally eat from
(all the other plates mismatched)
All down the long La-la-loo
And beyond, the schoolroom
With blackboard chalk and discipline
And the world, my kazooland,
The stores and the taverns,
And then the home of a sudden friend,
With hollow velvet chairs in lace
Collars, the whorl of the china
Cabinet, collection of bone dogs,
The whirl of that frame apartment
House, the La-la-loo place
the deep Wor-Wah

Concentric: The Window
--to Karen Armstrong

I am kneeling in a white square room where the air brings
A chill to my shoulders. My knees hurt a little. I am peering
At the stained glass overhead as it lights onto the floor
Before me in a borealis patch of shell, a mother of pearl spill
On the marble floor. I have left home. This is the convent
Vision of my childhood. I am nineteen. A virgin. I follow
The Christ. Most of all, however, contrary to Ma Mère's
Injunctions, I follow the light: the midnight blue that gleams
Like the Washable Blue of my Waterman fountain pen, the
Crimson as red as the flow of the monthly rags I wash
In the laundry house, the steam rising with the travail
Of women's eggs, lost and falling as if down this chapel wall.
There is an inky yellow, too, the color of forsythia or art-clay
From long ago Saturday afternoons, green and shiny as
A polished leaf. I join with the colors, mingle with them.
I am without boundary and the light comes in, plays with me.
I see the beech tree dancing outside the stained window
Above the altar. It calls to me, and I enter the tree beyond
Color, beyond my own sound, far beyond my own body,
My rumbling belly, out onto that swirling rim

What You Mean to Me

Honestly
I've never seen (the likes
Of) you
Sitting there
Warm smile
All suppleness
And yeasty grace
Strong hands molding
My (con) – (af) fections
Hold me in those
Strong hands
The sponge taking hold
I can feel this small loaf
Expanding
My bread rising
As you sit
In that exquisitely
Plumed Victorian chair,
Dark mahogany

Soyez Sage
"the light of truth's high noon is not for tender leaves."—
Gautama Buddha

Be careful of the light
(wear sunglasses)
its wisdom
not for the uninitiated
(wear shades)
(darken the pigment of your eyes)
(pull out your visor)
(wear a cap)
then look below
into the pool, Narcissus
let the sunbeams filter
over the deep
see the dappling effect
throw in the small stone
of your soul
let it ripple
as light plays
like fairies on dark water
now take in the sunned fluid
quench your thirst
one warm sip after another
to penetrate,
take in the light
incorporate
(now take off your visor
and your blinders)
let the light shine out
from your body, your eyes
then face the truth
sizzling in the skies

Budding: the Song

In memory there is bridal wreath
In pelvis and in bone
The little children playing
Near the river's stepping stone
All the backyards crying
And the muddy lots
Can never still the sobbing
Of neglected little tots

So as I see the swaying
On the bush today
Of snowballs or of bridal wreath
I feel the need to say

Memory is the answer
In all their history
The sounding of buds
Against the house
Will lend its urgency

For without the bud
As victor, without the seed
As flower, we remain
The little children
Lost and caught within that hour....

Fronds

All life is poetry, the gathering
Of powers, words the conveyance
Towards clearer silhouettes

In my journey toward the center
I meet you on the rim
And the world is spinning
And spinning, a bright spot
Of blue amid the stars

And I find your heat to be settling—
A still stream: warm water
On the planet: green fronds
Growing nearby

One

One is never enough:
One apple,
One kiss,
One field,
One book

Only the lone encampment
Where I gather with you:
Holding your arms,
That is enough
Under the embracing hemlock

Like the home of my grandmother
This cottage will be enough
Living in your smile,
Tonguing your luscious mouth

But one smile is,
Again one kiss is,
Not enough

The Colors

I began by painting the mountains,
The silk of tempera, the drip
Of watercolors heightened by rain

Down by the pond my toes pressed
The raw points of sandals, I was
Trying too hard, but now the hills
Were choreographing themselves,
Their nightly dance, their dusk-
Time swelling

I started, standing up their curves
On tiptoe, startled, still, then kicked
Off whatever was cumbersome:
The mountains were dancing
In the watery filter—my hands
Were free now to paint or not to—
I let go because now the mountains
Were painting me

Same Day, Different Tune

The mountains are painting me
I am painting the mountains
The bottom of mountains pale
The tops deep red, crimson,
Camel, and brown the bottom
Of mountains, and gold
The base of hills, the base
Of hills circular, full circle,
I wander around the mountain,
The road a wide ridge breathing

Locomotive

I was never settled, not as a girl
Or a young woman, not as
A young mother or the mother
Of teens. Always the earth
Sounded under me like
A gigantic trackless train
Rumbling, its unmerciful
Influence my soul, its lust
The only tributary, my only
Refreshment feeding and
Feeding, relentless energy.
Now I am an old woman,
Hair white, face soft.
I am, like my cat, centered
And gentle, needing much
Petting and the dailiness
Of selected toil, some
Slow discrimination.
Bright and bent, these feelings
Settle on my yard like snow

Six O'Clock

My father stood in the faltering
Lamp glow of the October sun,
His mechanic's fingers scarred
And bent, purple in the light,
His green workman's pants
Sagging at the seat and he
Cheshired that fake smile
I'd come to know, there
Were so many teeth in it,
So many sadnesses and
Missed joys, he held up
A quarter in the air, and
The sun spanked it gold,
Blinding it, extended
From his palm like
A St. Christopher's medal
Or a St. Jude's pledge,
This shiny token, its
Rays pelting me.
"Here", he said,
"Hurry up, take this,
this is for you."

Witness

"The hollow/silence I love grows wider and wider. Long/
after everyone is gone, I stand in a small/pool of
moonlight from a high window, making/no sound, making
no shadow." "Someone You Don't Know", William Stafford

I missed that eclipse three nights ago,
The one so heralded, lunar, the one
We won't see again until 2010. The
Night seemed perfect but the clouds
Imprinted themselves over that round
Mandala, buffeted it like dry ice,
Puffing themselves up as if they
Were, after all, more mystical.
Later, I'd watch clearly as the silver
Disk sunk to bob and spin behind
The darkened fingers of trees, her
Face open, as if with buoyant
Questions, her celebration
Solitary, unmasked, as if she
Sashayed unchased through
Lonelier heavens, wilder dreams

Trust

This is what I know about trust:
It is hanging your belly
On someone else's arm,
Letting your legs go limp
In the presence of that beloved
There is no journey
Like the voyage
That is about confidence
Your hot cheek
Lies flat against
The knuckles of someone
Else's desire, your sweat
Your drool, leave a puddle
Of sweetness on the one
You are imprinting:
No baby is aware
Of what it means
They just give over
Offer up belief without knowing:
But now that you know
What this lazy lethargy is
You can really hang in there
Truly trust; having faith
Suspends all other beliefs,
Those based on fear
Or skepticism

The Monk with the Guesthouse

He loomed quietly in the chill room
Set the papers burning in the fire
Had place mats circling the round tables
While his cats surveyed the grounds,
While does pranced in the scant trees

He was a cook, a minister to those who came
Had once been a narcotics deputy, but
Left young, an early retirement, to entire
Himself in these woods, in these redwood
Homes that once belonged to an oil magnet

His ads were quiet, in local papers,
The place called Hilltop, and the price
So affordable who would not come, just
Curious from busy roads or quiet, the farmer
And the city worker, crawling up the high
Hill in the encroaching darkness

Waiting to know the owner,
To be known, to set up camp
In the unclaimed universe of
Chickadee, jay, the open
Hands of St. Francis

The Decadence of Roses

And so the body opens:
In June there is always
This sweet budding
And the wind's fragrant
Unwinding, leaving petals
Overripe at the base
Of bushes yellow, magenta,
Coral: this luminous
Decadence, this unfurling
After the initial flower

Near graduation,
The velvet pieces float
Like bright balloons
Towards ground's open mouth,
Feed on earth's hunger,
Give witness to the lightness
Of love's real touch,
To kiss the world,
To let it be

Now

Queen Anne's Lace is here now
And now is not yesterday:
Queen Anne's Lace is jovial,
Rambunctious, oh, Queen
Anne's Lace is art! Once
Considered gothic, Queen
Anne's Lace is now modern
As a baby's ear, it is a chapel
Punctuated with a deep central
Drop, a blood-raspberry dimple,
The hum of August

Queen Anne's Lace on the breeze
Is a chorus of school girls caroling
To the noonday sun, saluting
The oak leaves overhead
Like future lovers. Queen
Anne's Lace is never retiring,
But bounces back, a healthy
Nipple under the finger. Queen
Anne's Lace glides under the digit
Of wind, transformed in the sound

Queen Anne's Lace is not so
Much an energy as the texture
Of a dry summer aging into fall,
The lazy circular dusty path
To Buffalo Creek. If a stone
Could be whatever it wanted,
It could not be Queen Anne's Lace,
For Queen Anne's Lace is buoyant
And free, a feather always slant
On the breath of god

"Tell the truth and tell it slant,"
Emily Dickinson says, and I say,
Tell yourself each morning, even
In purple fall and snow-streaked
Winter, This Day carries the truth
Of Queen Anne's Lace, This Day
Is a basket overflowing

West Seneca, New York: Charles Burchfield Nature Center

"Stand Here,
(So that all you were can come back slowly.")
--William Stafford

Oh ground, sustain me with your jewelweed,
The scent of mint on your strong hands,
Buoy me in a frilly pasture, the open meadow
Of schoolgirl petals. All summer, Buckhorn
Sumac, pods the color of blood, dip pensively
Over Buffalo Creek, and the creek is the gold
Of ribbon candy poured between split trees,
Barren rock: beyond the blue chicory see stalky
Wildflowers, a menagerie of bee balm, then spikes
Of zebra grass. Oh, I say, let this friendship
Continue, like loosestrife composing itself,
Long fronds, or as the white water does,
Chasing its own bubbles, let the hillside
On the other shore remain to me one single
Eye shining from the dewy grasses, tilting
Its short furrowed brow

Charles Burchfield Nature Center

Meteors

What happens when meteors
Fall from a sky dark as midnight
When sense leaves the body
Rising like steam to greet
The earth's rock shower?
What happens when two worlds
Collide, sense and land
Fire and stone, a stormy salute?
And when, on this special night,
When none of it is sun, when
Cloud covers the event, will we
Be surprised from our beds
With earth's gentle booming,
The quickening in the air?

Previously published in Buffalo News

Niagara

It is the end of summer:
There are dark red butterflies
On the river and the river
Continues its own running
Blue, against the cattails,
Banked stones, its movement
To the right, as it pushes
Towards the Falls

Feel yourself move, then
In the current's rush:
You who look out onto
The water, it is not
The river that moves
But you, racing on land
You, who are standing
Still near the river

Shadow

Elsewhere in the city a shadow dwells
The chiseled-ness of the real, the sultriness
Of hidden. On a gray morning you see
The lilacs pop over onto the stucco'd wall
Blooming, not innocent, ripe and yielding,
They are humming as they pierce the air

An Irish Epitaph

I was in many shapes before I was released:
A daughter of doom stirring the pots
While my sister studied damselflies in the sand,
A slender, enchanted wood where rocks walked,
Scraping gold from the trees. I was a bright ring
Around your heart before you were born, a bridge
That spanned islands, mounds of bluebells, seas.
I was a dolphin leaping over the wildness
Of water, I was the somersault in air

If We are Irish, If We are Strong

These messages were ours:
We called them telepathy—
A raised eyebrow, an insolent
Grin, two baudy breasts
Packed into a rosy blouse
Called cleavage, the secret
That nobody talks about
For years but one that's
Felt across the table
Like a fork in the hand,
Concrete as the tomato
On your sandwich, the one
Sliding out like a broken
Vow from just under
That gigantic piece
Of Boston lettuce—
A plate plunked down
With vengeance, a
Single flower, dry
As chicory, placed
In a lonely bottle, the
Touch of two fingers
On a baby's cheek.

**"*So what did you do
today?*"** becomes
The question, and
The answers begin
To take their crude
And silent, or whimsical
Forms. ***If I cough,
would you please forgive
me?*** It all means something
After all, the umbrella
Left dripping in the hallway,
My boots pointing in
Opposite directions

Genius

William Carlos Williams, "Danse Russe",
NY: New Directions, 1988

I was a happy genius then, the child said, precocious,
Typing at my computer, composing music for my violin,
Playing with my King Charles terrier.
I squinted towards
His body in that shadow, said nothing,
Though intrigued by his words, his passion,
Its sweet envelope of sound, its tone like the
folding of eggs and flour and honey

All I saw then was a corridor of trees,
Marching back to generations, hovels, caves,
The center of the earth, halls of rivers,
Floods of meaning and invention, hills of trust,
Skies like wide observation

I remember facing west one day in my
Girlhood mudpile. On my knees,
How the river leaped toward sun in twilight,
I could see it from my house three blocks
Away, the sun and the Niagara River,
Then the luminous peach ribbon
In between, my eyes opening and closing to
That amazing light

Holiday

Inside, outside
Warmth and cold
Turkey on the sideboard
Corn stuffing steaming
The air is full of cranberries,
Joy, the light of candles
Cradles the table around
Our down-turned eyes,
Just as the late afternoon
Sun dwindles in fingers
Of lavender and rose.
November is the mourning
Month: goodbye to fall:
Bare maple branches saluting
Winter, roasting the acorn
Squash

Ten

What a cold Christmas that was,
No socks in Grandma's kitchen but
The wanting, wanting, the hunger
Glazed cherries on the cake
A hot mug of tea, butter melting
In a bowl, but still I would
Ignore my cold feet, as they
Played on the floor, and one
And only presence in the room
Created heat in me, my peasant
Grandma, black Irish, her hair
In a stark plait down her back,
My little toes etching out
The chair rungs, my knees
Jiggling beneath my new
Flannel gown, the one
With pink roses. But!
All to myself, I hummed,
Her! My soulmate!
All to myself!
My grandmother hugged
Me with her wide hands
Tossed a thin blanket
On my waiting shoulders

Thinking about Georgia O'Keeffe

1.
Someone told me Georgia went to Amarillo
Living out her mother's stories of old
Cowboys, wide skies and the plains
So vast the grass would whisper
Mostly the land opened out from
One's feet in open progression
Toward the horizon, she loved
The mad wind merging with
The road in daily walks when
She stared hard at what
Was limitless: the airy plains
To her a vast ocean, an inner
Landscape, a place for personal
Ancestors, their bones

2.
Later, she'd say, "Where I come from,
The earth means everything. Life
Depends on it." And I want to be
Intimate with this space, not
The narrow streets of New York
City, but this. This place

3.
It was a perilous descent:
She and her sister, Claudia,
Each holding the end
Of a big stick, would climb
Down the rocks in total
Darkness, a night feel,
A passion for the canyons
That kept them hours
From sleep. Georgia
Would learn to abstract
By contrasts: "junipers,
Wild plums, grapevines
And cottonwoods,
Against the hot red
Of sandstone"

4.
Found poem:
"I had nothing but to walk
into nowhere and the wide
sunset space with the star"

5.
Found poem:
"I sat on the fence for a long time—
just looking at the lightning—"

6.
She was so strong
In her sense of things
That she could mold
The sky, swim expanses
Of mountains or wide
Plains, it was she
Perhaps, more
Than Columbus,
Who would discover
America, her own
Heartbeat in these
Hardened rocks

(Inspired by <u>O'Keeffe and Texas,</u> by Sharon Udall
(San Antonio: Harry N. Abrams, Inc, Publishers, 1998)

A Certain Slant

What slant brings us through
These winter afternoons?
What angle each day
Chisels like beach glass
On the gray sands covered
With rocks of ice and the
Invading lake? How do
We solve the winter riddle?

Cooking

"Dart throwers make the best cooks...they know how to
concentrate."
Jennifer Sears, "A Slight Change in Tuesdays", Fence, NY,
NY: Winter/Spring 2006.

If aim amounted to anything, I'd be the best chef
imaginable,
Targeting whole eggs into a crockery bowl on the way
To their perfect cracking, golden yolks displayed like
Monuments, perfect mothers, in their tiny space,
The whisk on the sideboard at the ready, a little
Soldier of circumstance

But here I am, the queen of stir-fry and broken
Parts, looking for love behind the range
In the most unfriendly of kitchens: only here
The counter is made for giants, its height
Brushing the contours of my breasts
As if an aberrant lover, my nose close
To the herbs of honor: cilantro, cinnamon
And another C-word: cardamom

I've never joined a dart club but was
Good at hoops once upon a time
Before the other girls reached past
My tiny height, then I couldn't even
Guard, and that has been my story,
Always frothy, never taken seriously:

I think I'll put my money on desserts.

Herself at Harvest Moon

1.
Moon weather
Yet people are pointing
Saying what's real to them,
The lake stretches
Out to join the river,
This is vice-versa!
And so she goes
Leaping to try
The hat on, suit herself

2.
Forgive me, you know how
I feel, forgetting to laugh,
I just hang around, small
Kisses, the touch that shakes
The breath, leaving me dissolving

3.
Beauty longs itself into memory
Working the edge, the double knot

4.
Light makes messy what is
Abandoned, frightened: it
Is high and green, lonely
Transparent, subtle slip
No shade pastel

5.
Never here, there already
Yet how quickly soon strongly
Yesterday: luck today, so lucky,
Love brought her home,
Opened the door

Intrusion

Inspired by William Stafford's "People of the South Wind",
first lines of each verse, from <u>The Darkness around Us</u>,
NY: Harper Collins 1993

1.
One day the sun found a new canyon
Oblivious to heat, it formed each
Crevasse as if with a finger, crevice
Upon crevice, water-full

2.
Your breath has a little shape
On these colder days—like smoking
From a fat cigar, your lips formed
In a circle

3.
Sometimes if a man is evil his breath
Smells like those old cigars,
A form of death, a nightmare
You can't quite remember, yet

4.
You know where the main river
Lies—and how it pushes you down
To the Falls, its brightness traveling
North

5.
When you cross that land the sandbars
Aid you, but they will not prevent
The current, and where the future
Flows

Ishtar

Oh, light of the world, Ishtar,
You are alone the Star, you
Are Esther, the Goddess Har,
Compassionate prostitute, you,
Speaking through senses,
Now say, "In the brilliant
Heavens...." in lips she is sweet,
Life is in her mouth, she is
Aphrodite, Kore, Cybele,
She is the lover, Mary
Magdalene. And all
The clouds bow down,
And the heavens shine
Like granite, topaz,
She is, up from earth,
Chrysanthemum, she
Is the raw wind, she
Is the darkest night
That assails the trees,
And finally, she is
November

Mercy Beaucoup: All Language
--to our leaders before wartime

It is the languages we speak, formidable,
That carry us on equal wings: new,
I'm a lark, you are a dove, and in this
Common language no hawks are found,
But only skyvaults and volleys, peaceful
Words carried across air waves, now
I am digging out my short wave radio,
Listening for the world's common cry,
Longing for the things we carry together,
What we laugh about, the sights of home
And sea, the turf fire and the mandolin.
And words, our languages, all change
The meanings somehow, not one alike,
In each we live alone, isolated in this
House of Babel. And you, if you are

An insider, if the culture belongs
To you, if yours seems the only tongue,
May have the arrogance to dictate
Your ways to the world, to demand
The earth's allegiance, you with
Your little shoes and your pride
As large as gunboats....but
I hope you won't. I know
Your intuition will tell you how
To speak with others, and gently
Unravel your intentions, your
Pockets full of wilderness and peace,
Merriment and the green humility
Of earth

Mirror

Inside there is a deep wanting: every day
During my bath I layer my fingers along the inside
Of my soapy arm, searching for something,
The deep blue vein that recedes in ocean,
The Anais or woman-place inside the seam
Of my body, the steamy tension of wanting
A joyful lover to seek me out, to kiss me
Along the pleats of my own secret map,
The unfolding of the gathered places, yes,
That is what it is, a perfect unfolding
Of all that has been pent up, covered,
Guarded, all that now like seeds springs up,
New and tendrilled, that wants to grow
And climb like morning glory

November

1.
These are trees mystical, green
Needles against the sky, pointed
Firs lined like crayons along
The water, a rim, a porcelain cup
Of verdant tea, these are November
Songs, rhythms that please bare
Ground, these are our stories, all
Thirteen, this is the universe
As we know it

2.
Yesterday, the maples hung
Their locks, bright redheads
Down to ground, as if washing
Their hair, the wind moved
Branches through their fronds,
Industrious fingers, washing,
Then rinsing, in November rain

3.
Tell me what is so important
About this particular autumn,
Is it the chiseled gate that
Closes on the forest malachite,
Or the bright one, pastel, that
Shows itself, a large door onto
The wide snow-swept winter?

The Map of Sadness

"Because I keep meeting sadness...even in my
soup...I've run away to a forest that's off the
map." Gloria Fuertes

She said sadness pursued her to an island that she'd
chosen:
She called and called to each person by name, anyone
Who'd tried to lose their essence in a leaf, a dog, a stone

She said come to me when everything sickens you,
Then you will find me whole and innocent, a wild pariah
Away from everything the world wants

Yes, you will find me strange. More important,
You will come to me in a language we both
Can speak: you see, I am, at last, honest:
I live my life like a snake: many skins

Seven: The Enneagram

It's an outgoing number, the one
In the Enneagram, my personality,
Seven, the one that absorbs everything:
Tries everything, investigates
The city, every street, is social,
Juggles seven balls while tromping
On its own interior self

Seven doesn't like to be alone
But it is the work of seven to face
The zero in herself, that hollow
Pool, to swim in it, to be drawn
Down into a lonely city,
The dark cave to view the empty
Factories, to forget the social tete-
a-tete, the luncheon or the disco bar

Seven speaks to herself harshly,
Then runs away, seven is an outside
Self speaking to the inside, lisping
You are always trying to be a sofa
When you long to be a chair.
If seven were a painted woman,
Could live beyond the age of sixty,
She would turn the flag at the top

Of her singular self backward, read
Books like <u>Small is Beautiful</u>, sit
In the garden on a lump of sod
Viewing a perennial, enjoy the silence
Of her length, and remembering,
Witness the old breath: a sail
Out on the water

Simplicity

Dee-Dee was seeking a quiet simplicity.
Something on the order of beauty.
Her Buffalo friend had said in the north simplicity
Is not lush, tropical, a plate of Florida fruit at the end of
The day, Not a t-shirt and a pair of luau shorts.
In Buffalo, simplicity in March is the ancient wisdom of
Trees, topless, bereft of leaves.
Through trees' empty branches you can see the light,
Wait for the sun like a sentinel on the hill.
In Buffalo you wait for simplicity. It is a lonely task and
You are willing to do it, to wait for spring, to patiently
Meditate as your life comes to you. Fatalistic, the wait.
But deep. Marjorie lived the life of an Eskimo, jaundiced,
Bone-white, leaden, heavy in the winter, licking up fat
From her plate, slathering butter on her bread

Yes

Yes, she told me, beauty is simplicity. She was calling
Me from her bathtub in Hollywood, Florida. Standing
In the tub gave her the coolest allusions, she said.
She came home late at night and peered out from
The bathtub at the stars, counting their number,
Perceived them, felt their persistence, had a little cry.
She didn't want to disturb her lover, just take a little
Time to herself, a little heart-to-heart with the Goddess.
Was that a cottonwood tree or a banyan? Did Marian
Anderson sing "His Eye is on the Sparrow" or was it
Odetta? She had just closed up the bar-restaurant
Where she worked, collected her tips. Now she
Was home from the wars, just another Crocodile Dundee.
And the breezes filtered into the moist bathroom
From beyond the sheer curtain. The breezes whispered
To her their own beauty in the night

Buffalo Winter

Whenever Marj brooded of her own death, she felt
It could happen in winter. If she was ill and
Beyond redemption, she would go out into
Her yard, would make snow angels all over
The earth, the small plot she lived on. Meantime,
Just waiting for spring, she felt the depth of living,
Of patience in her bones. She could wait for any-
Thing here on this rim next to Canada. She could
Wait for a lover, for Spring, for herself. She could
Welcome the loneliness of winter's end as if a long
Lost friend, a fellow sufferer. She would pull it
Like a familiar afghan around her shoulders. ***This,***
She thought, as she began to fall into slumber,
Is how you come up with truths. Of nature, of life,
Of familiarity and devotion

Snow Promises

Snow is falling today, chill wind
Takes it in a far loop from the park,
And pours it here, on this little
City street, under the lamp's glow

Call it charming or inevitable,
In Buffalo, the snow is with us
Here in February, you must
Embrace it as a long lost friend,
One come back to fill you in,
To encompass you, to be
Your family

Each day I thank its white
Reflection, its promise of light
Bounced back in all directions,
Much better than the gray
Drizzle of November, this is it,
The white panorama, the
Clouds draped back, the theater
Curtain plied, all actors, squirrels
And nuthatches, the ancient woman
Clutching her deep wool bag

Just Before Thunder

The spider spins her crystal web over the hostas
And up the wooden fence where I watch her sit
In that crystal sweat-drop of humidity. Of course
I am talking about July, the burgeoning drone
Of insects and the spiky Scottish thistles
On impatient days. But it is the patience of spiders
That invites me, pulls me, it is the tenuous rest
And arduous work of a Friday afternoon,
It is a spider on a hosta leaf, that is all
And everything

Sally Johnson's Apple Tree
(from her photograph)

I am looking at the apple tree
And all the grasses reaching,
The bright sky, almost white
Behind the floating orbs of apples,
The apples dancing, hynotized
In the morning light, the crate
On the left waiting to be filled.
There are apples bobbing
In the gentle breeze, a child's
Party game, and one or two
Pointing out like suckling breasts.
This, then, is an enchanted tree,
Immeasurably itself, swinging
In the mild air, held staunchly
By its wooded trunk, thick
And solid. If this tree could
Talk, she would say, "Eat me,
Drink me. I'll be all to you,
Great nourishment, profound
Celebration. Finger paint
With my juices, this is life,
Consumable"

Last Sight

I used to go there just before dream,
The place on the porch where the wind
Chimes clamored, the small corner
In the cellar where the cat communed.
Day followed day and still no news, no
Epiphany but always meditation,
Swimming the laps, then floating
Keening on bad days
I had thought our lives there would
Last forever, small children,
The warm touch of your hands,
Largely resting on my shoulders.
Now I look out a blue door, the
Small view succinct and specific,
A binocular held backwards

Want

She let go of all expectations,
Of wanting the winter air
To feel abundant, as yellow
As summer, the taste
Of brownie like salt,
A scent of pretzel
Sweet on the lips

She is living in this moment,
Not the next, her cheeks
Feel the winter's chill,
They don't gloss over it

Outside, she can stand
Still as a snowman, never
Complaining that her nose
Is long, her eyes
Glazed as coals....

Nor will she lament
That she stands upright
And silent while the winds
Whirl. She is humming.
Let the coals take it in,
Glisten

Erratic

Someone said she was erratic, but she never paid
Attention to those words, not what to name her cat
And if not Snow, SnoYin, her cat's name, and that
Little animal so gentle and so defensive, so ballsy
And so hissy under her coverlet, that little pussy
So pissy yet so darling, so definitely in the mode
Of all cats, all cats feline. And now she kept on
Thinking, she, adding to the little file on this hissy-
Pussy, should she add or delete, get rid of the
Little feline, she, like Gertrude, so strong on
The outside, but nothing without an Alice, no,
Nothing without the calm gentle voice that could
Stay her, who could make her rest, who could take
The leonine grin out of her soul and put back
The little goldfish, flipping and dipping in her
Own proximate and little bowl:

Too much wackiness going on in the new house,
And now her friend had given her a Matisse and
A Miro! and also a Calder. But she was a shout
And a calamity, and everything she had done
To improve her lot seemed harder, the stakes
Seemed harder and more difficult and she
Didn't know what to do. She was growing
Older and more real, more complex and more
Exhausted, she was like Colette, a cat on her
Arm (or under her bed) and the feline within
More nervous, more destitute, more concerned
And more alone. And she felt so frightened
By her leavings, more than her beginnings,
Always the leavings were the hardest. Because
They made her trust herself less and less,
Like a hissy-pussy always up late and working
On things but scared and destitute and needing
Direction and needing someone to be a rock,
Or herself to be a rock and change the
Direction of her all-overness

It was this all-overness that was, as someone
Had said, the sign of the intuitive, always the
Uncovering of this and that, always seeking
Out the potential, the possibility, always
Kissing the unknowable, the unobtainable,
Always dancing with the devil, and always
Playing out torch songs on the dance floor,
Always looking for a friend, and having one,
Never looking for a lover, but knowing the
Next one just around the bend. And she
Described herself to herself and then knew
Herself to be thinly disguised, a little
Hysterical girl, just Gretel, dashing across
The road again and again to find Hansel,
His eyes caught like a deer in the headlights
Coming through the Darkness

And she sought out the rock and knew she'd
Find it, knew she'd know the rock if she'd
Only sit under the black thorny bower
Of the hissy-pussy tree

Seasons

Flow into me, says Loss
Come to the basement of reason
Where all your feelings dwell

This is the house of dreams
The pull of tide, this is the season
Of forgetting

Come into the water and merge
With the moon as it glimmers
Over the deep, opaline

This is your spirit's divining rod,
The tool of your heart's wandering

Say Something Surreal:

"Cavalcade, how lips stick
Pressed to popsicles,
How the whirlpool carries
You in, whipping you
Round and round till
You're a shorebird, picking
Up French fries and cigarettes
In the moist sand, imprinting
Your small forked foot there,
Bella Abzug would be proud,
She laughed out loud at each
New day, wearer of many hats,
Big-fisted, bellicose Bella, I
Want her life to lean again
Into kind winds, pushing
The willow past its own
Envelope, a sculpture
In the garden, a hot
And violent fire, no rabbit
Can hop into the square
Courtyard without
Concentration, the labyrinth
Of New Orleans some
Lavender door and now we
Are at The Bottom of the Cup
Tearoom...."

The Sounds of War

Do you hear it? The sounds of war?
Those sentiments that are brewing?
Our President bought the election,
Now he buys the world, 2 cents
A barrel, a dollar a soul, now
We call him tyrant and angrily
Bow before him, we will hit
Our heads against concrete, we
Will eat nails, we will kiss the rat-
Infested caves of doom before
We believe him, he is knock-kneed
And weak-willed, he who kicks
With a pointed Texan toe the family
Jewels of everyone in the world,
Yelling: This is a boy's fight, but
I will gladly take your wives or
Children, your cousins and fathers,
Your mothers and brothers, and yes,
All the others, I talk of bridges
And healthcare, AIDS networks on
The earth: I am here to build bridges,
Yes, links, please believe me, they
Are all tinker toys to me, as you are,
And I will blow them up: Take me,
Take me, before I take you

How Grief Travels: Poems about 9/11

The Moment

The moment it's started, it's already done,
The master said, the master of no-think,
No-thing, the Zen breather of creation.
If the paint doesn't take you in, the paper
Does. It sponges you full, alive, becomes
An entrance way into ocean waves. One
Circle precedes the other like the loop
Of breath, a cell, an ovary, all are spinners,
Circular, life on life, again, again.

It only took one stroke for thousands to die
That evil September, but for the dying it was
Already done, they opened their eyes, squinted
To see and the bright light shattered them,
No pain, no knowing, and they entered
The realm of the unknowable, that secret stroke,
The calligraphy of wisdom, wet, black, finished.

How Grief Travels: Poems about 9/11

Babel

What circle brings us here at the foot
Of the great tower, Twin Trade, as it
Dissolves, and the rooms fall liquid,
The structures erode like a great
Theater curtain, a veil or a tear?
Why does hate fly in the face of brothers
And sisters? We are all in this little land,
The world, we are all here living, questing,
And hope sends us wheeling into new skies.
Always, in history, progress impedes us:
In the technology of weapons few can say
"I am", hard to grow when zealots and
patriots will call themselves a nation:
margins, boundaries, and the machinery
of war. One language will help us now,
if we are willing to speak it.

How Grief Travels: Poems about 9/11

America

The wanderer returns to lands unlived in, the place
Where the ancestors came from, their faces bright
With promise.

Now America is a wanderer looking for a home
In the wildness of a rural land, an old truck farm,
A harvest of vegetables, the vase that hides
The ashes of lineage.

Now America, once so new, not a little naïve,
Looks for the old country, seeks the values
Of struggle and purity, we have evolved only
A little, knowing we are not central to the world,
Only human, only ourselves.

Today I saw a woman who came out alive
From the Towers. She was being interviewed
With her husband, who described her as
Once vivacious, independent, lively. Now
She avoids tall buildings, cannot return

To work across the bridge, won't sleep
Without a light. Now all her friends must come
To her, descending their stairs from lofty heights
She will no longer travel. Somehow her fears
Move, as wide and deep as her grief: she says
Now she cannot be alone, and I think, **yet she is**

**She is now a wanderer, longing to return
To lands unlived in, she is looking for the old
Country, the place where the ancestors came
From. She is looking for a home in the wildness
Of her land**

How Grief Travels: Poems about 9/11

After: Airborne Pieces in NYC

Before you know what happiness really is, you
Must enter a deep garden where white butterflies
Live, soaring between kale and carrots and cabbages,
Testing the bright cutting essence of vegetable,
The taste of earth and acrid sky.

And, as you enter, you must notice every blade of grass
And how they lean lime and yellow at the base
Of hemlocks, thinning out on their trail to the trunk,
Encircling the tree in the mud.

When winter comes, the roads will look sweeter for
The snow that covers gravel and scattered branches.
And the trail then to anywhere will be white, calling
To you, telling you where to place your feet.

I have learned that a white butterfly can lead you
When you don't know where to find a path. Those
Resonating butterflies, all origami, cheered the
Children of Nagasaki, a real one will push you
To enter the core.

This must happen before you enter kindness, before
You can know just what is happy, how friendly
The earth is.

How Grief Travels: Poems about 9/11

Comfort

I am remembering where comfort lies. It lies
In the cooking smells of my kitchen, the scents
Of cilantro, garlic, lemon balm, the thrill
Of coriander, a hint of sage. It lies in the wide
Chair where I can curl up with my cat, a book,
My writing. Comfort is the window in this
Warm room, a porthole into the ocean
Of world, wide trees where love is, bending.
Comfort is volition, a world at peace, knowing
That human alignment, agreement, can make
It so. Comfort can be just that simple, whether
Or not the world is simple, comfort can take
You to the peaceable kingdom, to the land
Of let it be.

How Grief Travels: Poems about 9/11

Running

We race through these eternal nows, open,
Uncontained, until our history encodes,
Encloses itself in its own waterskin,
Lives its life. The life had been until
That war about promise and containment,
Hope and humanity. Later, it would be about
The veil: women veiled Arab and women
In American both, opening their feelings
And veiling them in a war some would
Pretend to love.

Meanwhile, the breadlines grew longer
In Afghanistan and America, little
Children looked out from oversized
Clothes with poignant eyes. Some
Said, look for the daystar across
The border to Pakistan. Others,
Stateside, cried, "Let's bomb
What is hidden: caves, crevices
In rock, let's root out the rats,
Taliban, so we can preserve
The nation." Food lines circling
The globe, a veiled Depression.
Warplanes overhead, condensation.

How Grief Travels: Poems about 9/11

Future

When you are focused, dominant
And proud, whether you say your
Rosary or bow to Allah, whether
You bike fast up the cold mountain,
And whether you ever finish
Your breakfast, slurping cereal,
Milk from your bowl

It's not that you can't write
Your own history, it's not that
You don't have a prayer: it's
Just the sudden jolt, a light
Hits and sends you like a
Shooting star, out and out,
Bright roads in the distance,
And overhead, trees.

Iraq War: More Poems

Imagine

Imagine the smell of the world's anger
Over rotting skulls that lie in fields,
Brains replete with knowledge and
Wisdom, future Einsteins and Joan
Of Arcs.

Imagine the stink of Baghdad burning,
And soldiers jutting about abruptly
Shooting others, saving themselves,
Then saving their fellows, thereby
Losing themselves.

There's a foment in this form
Of civilization that is so corrupt
There is no description, charred
Bodies, dead hearts, and all
The monuments broken, but
Still there is form, concrete
And gold.

Oh, the heart of the world
Is broken, it has no surface,
Just an empty room, a hall
Of mirrors, and wills
Unbending with principles

Compassion has the smell
Of wild orchids and hate,
The stink of cabbages
And blood.

Iraq War: More Poems

Wartime

From these drums in wartime,
We are chanting. The women
Are speaking again and again,
The trees know what we are
Saying, we speak with the words
Of nature not of law, the words
Of wildness and compassion,
We scream some sanity at least
To a government who cannot
See, those devoid of a heart that
Cares truly about one other
Heart.

Iraq War: More Poems

Consider

The snow, its crystal state,
It only moves when nature
Warms it, it actually provides
Us needed insulation
So in these times, does
Government consider itself
A buffer, a keeper of souls
And humanity, a voice
Calling, a sheltering sky?
There is one at the center
Of our government who
Would be king, his foot
A bloody imprint on the
World, this is not the nation
We hoped for, these are
Brooding, murderous skies,
Over a people asleep
In houses surrounded
By snow.

Iraq War: More Poems

Into the Creases
"Waistband slips into the flat pleat of seasons."
—Karen Lewis

A selfhood of nations slips through
The thinness of the wall
Government stops the news from leaking
While blood runs down the page,
Front page says our Predator shot
A missile called Hellfire: a car filled
With AlQueda....Second page byline
Quips about our new softer methods
Of war: "non-harmful" gases, valium,
Opium sprayed into crowds, and if all
Else fails, Multicultural Music! (**We
Just have to discern the culture**).
Soon we will be dealing with an old
70's déjà vu: the subliminals in
these messages to make the world
like us, at last to fall asleep on the
opiates of paid advertising, non-
working voting machines, crafted
elections, and fallen senators,
their powers taken by the Bush-mills
grinding all of us into their at once
haughty, then cynical, and utmost
faux pearls.

Shoes

I had wanted to walk in her shoes:
They laced up top and half-way to
Her knees, they looked TIME-
Consuming—oh, well, now I'm tired,
It's winter, I'm falling asleep

But then the dream comes back:
One spring in fifth grade on the play-
Ground, I tossed a basketball with
The beautiful Sharon McGinty, a
Fourth-grader, who wore the most
Delectable cranberry leather lace-up
Shoes I'd ever seen: deep and red
As port wine, glossed as high as
A fever, her little anklets tight
And pale, her feet bound in the
Most forgiving cowhide, it all
A mark of care and love, the
Exquisite way she carried herself,
The eternal way I'd noticed she
Was loved by her family. I vowed
To be like her, dark snapping eyes
Fringed in black lashes, a thick
Coil of black hair.

Later, at summer's end, just when a new
School year began, my mother took me
Down Grant Street, where I could buy
Any school clothes I wanted: a sweater,
Blouse and skirt, and of course, shoes,
Any outfit at Norban's, any pair of shoes
At Liberty's or Schiff's. I chose a flecked
Pleated skirt in pink gabardine and a pair
Of brown oxfords just like Sharon's
Cranberry ones.

We stood on the steps of school, waiting
For the doors to open, she a step below
Me. "Look, just like you!", I rhapsodized,
And Sharon stared and stared. "What?",
She asked, not getting it. "Me! Why I
Look just like you! Look at my skirt, my
Shoes!" (*I had already begun to wonder
If my skirt was in style*). "Oh, those
Awful shoes, I don't have to wear them
Anymore, they were for my flat feet."

When You're An Ordinary Child

Who wants to steal a dog,
The collie you see walking
On the street on Be Kind
To Animals Day, anyone
Would know you were
Growing up in a 4-room
Apartment, a cold water
Flat, your desire palpable,
No room for dogs

Surprisingly, your Dad
Says **Maybe we can
Keep her in the attic**
But already your stomach
Is flipping thinking of
The gorgeous beast
Surrounded by wasps
And heat of summer and
The frigid sheets on that
Upper clothesline
After frost

Beloved Cora, the old
Lady downstairs, cements
The deal: **You wouldn't
Want to take a girl's
Pet, now would you?**
She intones, with
Kind dark-brown eyes.
**I know the girl who
Owns the dog. You
See, the dog has
A collar, her last
Name is right here**

Last Lover

I am cutting a path now
Beyond violence and erosion
Beyond mind games
And serving you:
I serve myself now,
With pen and notebook
The gathering of women
And the breath, the
Ingathering of power
There are no gods here
Save me and the sweet
Process of existence
The clarity of the osprey
As she swoops and circles
Near the marsh
The hum of mosquitoes
As they rise up to multiply
Near swaying loosestrife
In the purple night

Perfect

I was born with most things
Angel wings for shoulder blades
Red, spikey hair to express
My devil, two parents who
Yearned toward each other,
They formed a leaning tree,
Books, and words, and mystery
Most of all these
But then the cutting away
Of spirit, being carefully formed
By careful hands
Who wanted to make me,
As girls should be,
Made right

History

In the hidden places are the moments
Of truth: when I gave birth
To my daughter's truth she mirrored
In bright lights with hair the color
Of tomato, when I opened the book
And saw her name, when I found
My own and knew I was a woman,
When love stole surprisingly in
The night and opened her story
On the moon-strewn sheets,
Whenever light breaks into the
Dubious crevices of this living
Breathing space, when real
Cracks through, this is the angel
Of history

She says Don't Look Back,
It is a widow's muse when you
Look back, it is dark veil
Over the oilcloth, it is
The candle's drip, it is
The place where the scent
Of incense walks into a room,
When you absorb it, the scent,
All about you is a garden,
Solomon's seal, African
Impatiens, Japanese iris
And bulbs will burst forth
From everyone's garden
And everyone is who you love

Does the angel of history
Come to touch you in the night?
Come to weave the disparate
Pieces in the garden, come
To soak you in a fine green mist,
The dark tropic of who you were
Once: a mere girl attached
To a string, attached to a bright
Kite in a golden field? Was the
Field dry then, without water,
Was the field full of poppies
Or the promise of summer rain,
And when you held yourself
Ever so minutely aloof, did
The voice come to you like
A cool well, did it whisper
"Here now, you are in this
Garden, grow now, be your
Own sister, write your own poem"

Cats

Cats can teach us everything, how timeless
The hours are, how playful the moments,
Tracing an air castle with an enlarged paw,
Then tackling and landing it, downing it
With each feeling until the castle comes
Back bobbing, a new country in the sea,
Boldt Castle among these Thousand Islands

Today

Today, "sitting in a sunny doorway": (Thoreau),
I watched time melt, the moments hot and fierce,
But limpid too, as perspiration on an arm, the
Wetness of a furrowed brow

These moments pass like heat
Like sunflowers bobbing, tall
Stalks, the end of cottage days,
The wide fronds of Queen Anne's
Lace, white pens on dark paper,
Their punctuation scratching
The dirt, the croak of tree frogs,
The hum of grasshoppers, dryness
Of sand paths to the beach

The Whales
  45 pilot whales were stranded on Cape Cod,
July 30, 2002

Here on the Massachusetts sands,
Dozens of whales lie like black signets:
Lost to consciousness, talismans
Suffering in a new climate, torpid
Seas.

They are venerable, these mammals,
Their wide blue eyes open, topazes
Toward a heaven oceanic, they
Have washed on shore, the lost
Ark.

I can see their vulnerability,
Large and wet on the bank,
Hosed down by the saviors,
Gently carried by mourners
Roping, then lifting the bier
Of a comatose stranger.
We are taking back
To sea.

Who will see us clearly
If they don't? I heard many
Of their kind swam here
As if with purpose, to deliver
The Earth to us, to show
We can endure.

One whale calls her name to us:
The World, the Body, and the
Grave. She is the womb,
The belly of the giantess,
She is cosmic night, dare
We go to her?

"I have made myself a tribe...."
Stanley Kunitz

Odd, the people I have come from
And return to, an olive temperament
Of skin, my grandmother's broad feet
Spread wide near the sandbox, the
Place where I could sift reality
Grain by grain near the house's
Fake brick siding, try a new song—
I was afraid then of the stillness
In me, a turgid pond, one of
Tranquil water, a place of lily pads
Holding themselves out like armchairs,
Frogs out-leaping each other, croaking
Their secrets better than I could mine

Tension was a fog that I lived in:
A mist that was cumulative, a voice
That couldn't be heard on wind. But
The wind was brave. And, if I could
But snowshoe in those elements,
Past copper factories and smoky stars,
To the edge of my city, I'd then look
Out and see the only world there was,
One half orange, an arc, a lighted
Hemisphere

Another Tongue

"Each word/has a crack in it/to show the strain
of all it holds/all that leaks away." "Second Language"
by Tess Gallagher, Amplitude, (St. Paul: Greywolf
Press, 1987)

This is what I don't write, the crack
In the world, the void in my stammer.
Each day the rain cleanses the synapses
Between words that might be spoken,
The weather shocks you with its own
Electricity. Today, at the school meeting,
A boy, nine, scruffy and soft as a bear cub,
With downy dun-colored hair, slides on
His chair: across it, frontwards and back,
Sliding this way and that, across his
Own truth. And none of us would ever
Know it, the secret buried within the
Vaults of him, entombed in the heart
Of Saint Agnes, and his green-flecked
Eyes, notations of hazel, delve deep
Into each person at the table with
A solid holding, as if to grab their eyes

Would be to yank their meaning and,
Once in a while, his lip would poke out,
Petulant, as when he pronounced his
Mother's name, accenting her unusual
Middle name, to make its significance
Even larger, her hold on him even more
Powerful. I felt I had encountered a
Small life raising itself in the forest,
Fuzzy, impetuous, wily, a Romulus or
Remus boy, both free and, mirrored,
Unfree, with guarded eyes and a million
Histories. "Tell me one of your stories,"
I said, "Just one of them." *Tell me*
About the time you went to the Emergency
Room when that girl you liked gave you
A tiny shell, and you inserted it deep
In your ear, needing to know the truth
Of oceans

Stallions

The stallions clouded the horizon
In that Mexican desert, they
Ran with the heat of the plains,
They harvested power, and
Snorted as they passed:

I had known them
In my dreams, they pulled
Me on ropes and chains,
They dragged me up from
Revery, from a just meeting
Of my mind, to know my
Arms, my elbows, the strength
Of my hands

I remembered then how I
Knew the energy of their haunches,
How like one crazed I too had
Been through deserts, plains,
How once upon a time in the very
Long ago I had been a mystical
Rider, I had been the horse, I
Had been the plain that at last
The rain had fallen on, the desert
In full mad bloom

Love

Love is a freewill offering
Like a gift at church,
A donation—
So, put a little
In my collection plate!

Baby, Let Me Make You Bouillabaise

Baby, let me make you bouillabaise—
It is the steamy heat of summer,
Let me lift lobster to your lips,
Those luscious chunks, let the shrimp
Shimmer in basil and saffron, let
The tomato be your very own seducer
And the sexiness of parsley pour
Like cleavage between your teeth.
And garlic! I want to coat your tongue
With huge cloves mixed with orange peel,
A dribble of olive oil, clams clinging
To their shells, trembling, as bright
As the heart that quickens

Gullah

The area was a low country boil, we moved
Sinuously in our canoe between the cotton-
Woods, we sought the Gullah and their
Songs, we sensed the villagers before we
Saw them strung out like snakes along
The banks of their encampment. We ate
With them and then they sang, their voices
Rising and rising, touching the stars and we,
Enthralled, touched each other light as
Fireflies, hearing the tree frogs hum under
Veils of Spanish moss

The men sang so deep as if from an aboriginal
Pipe and their voices blended up and up until
We saw them, two suns, one in the East
And one in the West, and we knew then the
Songs were over, and soon we'd book our
Passage back

Night

There's something about waiting,
Loving your vision, watching the trees
Billow in the dimming light outside
Your window as night falls

It is in the closing envelope of time
Where things grow more chiseled:
Objects are closer than they appear.
Hindsight is 20/20

This is what loneliness knows
And holds, the sweet treasures
Of the night, the soul
That fingers them for sustenance, a
Body that holds its own remembrance

Witness

In the heat of August afternoons
The old ladies told secrets
In humid circles about dead
Parents and husbands, taboo
Lines their children had crossed,
Race and gender, and how now
They understood, their feet
Contained still in the tight
Oxfords of their married lives,
But their bosoms heaving, loose
With the witness of all of it:
All things changed. All times
Were transient as they were,
The blooming of a tight red bud,
The fall of a brittle leaf, the
Drop of rain in the pond, the frog
That sang Alleluia there

Pine Cone

She was a pine cone, a little succulent pine cone,
Covered with a sweet shellac of resin, dew, she
Was a pine cone and when she made love to the
Loamy grasses that were between herself and
Earth she rode on them sweetly, subtly. She
Was a pine cone fallen from the tree towering
Toward a little patch of blue, her own brown
Woodiness a joy to her, she was a pine cone
Savory as air's salt, minty as the scent of trees—

She was a pine cone, she was a pine cone
Germinating on the viney curlicues of the forest,
She placed her portrait among all the woodsy art
Ever captured, she was however, no Vincent Van
Gogh, no Emily Carr, she was singly and simply
Only a pine cone.

And her singleness made her feel sublime, made
Her feel unique, supremely and uniquely delivered,
Sent, arrived, pushed, given birth to. Yes, she said,
I am a pine cone.

If

If the moon sails like a ladle
Over the simmering soup
Of the world, and if the earth
Pours out as nourishment
Piping tomato and corn
And bean, if blue sky
Sends wind to cool the soup
And if the tall wheat
Of Nebraska makes the bread
What else will we need?
Just soup, just bread.
And land and sky. Just
A small ladle of moon
Spinning by

Last Night

Last night, just near sleep
I saw her walking the tightrope
Between her work and home,
Stringing the ropes, cat's cradle,
Across her forehead, a hat,
Spare part, a wide band
In the heat, and she dripping,
Dripping down, between
Perspiration and the river,
Between the sunrise
And comfort there was
Always that heat, and today,
An unbroken band of gold
That makes breathless
Our friendship, our arms
Sticking to each other
On folding chairs

Perilously tucked into
The steamy granules
Of beach sand, the air
Like haze over our heads,
Our words formless, one-
Syllabled, drawling, our
Hands slowly expressing
Our droopy overladen thoughts

"It's the heat," we say

Who Can Understand?

I didn't know what made me strong,
Only the wind knew where the
Seeds would fly—then hope
Landed on my own tough
Ground

Enough water

Enough light

My fingers for the trowel
My own big arms to hold it

The End